Influencing and Interpersonal Effectiveness

**To the Point
Transformational Handbooks
for Business and Personal
Development**

 PUBLISHING

To the Point

Copyright © Jacqueline Mansell 2019
ISBN 978-1-9164398-6-3
First printed 2019
Published by FCM PUBLISHING
www.fcmpublishing.co.uk
All rights reserved. No part of this publication may be reproduced (other than purposes of review) without written consent of the publisher and or author

Also by Jacqueline Mansell

Resilience A Choice for Everyday Living
Bullying and Harassment of Adults

To the Point

Contents

Introduction 9

About 'To the Point' 13

Part 1.

Your capacity to influence

    We all have the power to influence others, we do it every day 15

    Recognizing that we are all actors in an on-going drama 23

    'Case in Point' Examples 37

Part 2.

Varieties of influence

    Summary of positive influencing skills ... 41

    Power 47

    'Case in Point' Examples 57

    Manipulation 59

    Persuasion and Proposition 67

Part 3.

Sphere/Circle of Influence

Understanding your sphere/circle of influence 75

Expanding personal influence 81

Part 4.

Influencing Techniques

Choosing to be assertive: The alternative options 93

Choosing to be assertive: Effective behaviour 107

Being a great listener 125

Questioning 135

'Case in Point' Examples 147

Building rapport 151

Proposition and persuasion 159

Information 173

Part 5.

Personal Positive Power to Create Influence

Character and charisma 179

Part 6.

Concluding the Influencing Process

Gaining commitment and handling objections..191

Disengaging and ending 203

Note...207
About the Author..209

To the Point

Introduction
Influencing and Effective Communication Skills

All of us are subject to the potency of influencing. For example:
- Following and joining trends
- 'Reality' TV and copying celebrities
- Being swayed by advertising
- Celebrity endorsements
- Reacting to the media
- Emulating role models
- *'Keeping up with the Joneses'*
- Keeping up with colleagues and acquaintance
- Being swayed or pressured by family, partners and friends

Equally, at the most primitive of levels our genes can serve to influence others. Our genetic predisposition to be a certain size, to be tall or short, to have different hair colour, eye colour etc. to lean towards different personality types or display particular traits and behaviours can all have an impact on how we are perceived. In turn this may moderate the behaviour of others towards us, impact upon levels of success during interactions and even affect our long-term relationships.

As sentient individuals we each have the potential to influence others. When carried out by example and with integrity, influence can be a powerful aspect of behavioural competence in the skills toolbox. On the other hand, if those who have been influenced believe they have been manipulated or abused by power there can be long term consequences such as anger, lack of cooperation, lack of trust and cynicism.

Influence can be wielded on a large scale and might be seen as spread across nations through propaganda and fear. Equally, influence can take place between two people, it might be experienced in a coercive relationship or in a gentler form in situations where one-person cares for another. It is a key skill relevant across many occupations from customer facing roles to positions of line-management and leadership. In getting things done influencing skills are fundamental both to managing upwards as well as developing relationships across networks to create strong bonds and seamlessly achieve results.

Even when things may seem overwhelming to a minority, without status or power and who seek to sway a majority, influence can prevail. The minority can demonstrate alternative viewpoints which may raise doubts or cause others to reassess their position. Even if effects are not immediately apparent influence can lie latent and manifest later as 'light-bulb' moments. In addition, as the world turns, and things change the minority view may be recognised as more realistic than the outmoded majority.

With these points in mind this book may be read as a birds-eye view or can be used as a practical resource with the contents actively applied in more intimate, every day or business settings.

The aim of this handbook is to:
- Explore the art and discuss methods of communication, influencing and persuading others in order to gain cooperation, support and commitment
- Enable readers to influence the achievement of successful outcomes while retaining the respect and trust of others

.

> "The outside influences are always pouring in upon us, and we are always obeying their orders and accepting their verdicts."

Mark Twain

About To the Point

'To the Point' are books, which have been developed and written with different readers in mind, but in all cases designed for practical and easy use. These quick to read behavioural skills handbooks encapsulate experience and knowledge drawn together throughout a career supporting the development of individuals and organisations.

The handbooks provide you with straightforward access to theories, ideas and frameworks proven to achieve results, account for behaviour and which can be integrated into everyday living.

The style of To the Point enables different levels of engagement at different points throughout:
- **Quotations** provide nuggets of good advice and information which have been neatly summed up by thinkers of the world.
- **Case study boxes ('Case in Point')** provide useful examples in a stand-alone format.
- **Highlighted key words (Flip-charts)** are presented as punctuation points with quintessential meaning
- **Bullet points** present a practical and succinct read

The handbook format and style of layout has great advantages as it eliminates the 'filler'. Meaning that it is very useful for busy people – the research has been done and you reach the 'gold seam' of knowledge immediately.

'To the Point' is ideal for:
- Individuals who would like to increase their personal knowledge and understanding
- Organisations who wish to provide tool books for managers and teams
- People who want to learn quickly
- Discovering ideas, information and concepts to provide a springboard to deeper study

Part One. Your Capacity to Influence

We all have the power to influence others, we do it every day…

"*You don't have to be a 'person of influence' to be influential. In fact, the most influential people in my life are probably not aware of the things they have taught me.*"

Scott Adams

Consider a baby, it babbles in what appears to be contentment and happiness and in response the carer makes a cooing sound or says words of encouragement.

The toddler adopts an angelic expression enchanting those around him/her who respond with cuddles.

A baby gurgles with delight as it is lifted up and down above the carers shoulders and so the carer continues to lift the baby high.

These types of scenarios were identified by the Psychologist John Watson as being game-like interactions where a baby realises that it can make the world respond. The baby and toddler learn through reinforcement the effect it's cries, expressions and behaviours have on those around her/him. In other words, even a baby has the capacity to influence.

The behaviours described are labelled as 'signals'.

Signalling can work one-on-one. It can also operate when any number of people, from two upwards synchronise their actions and coordinate their approach and behaviour to send out messages to others. On a large scale for example, consider the effect of a spectacle such as guards unified in their actions for the Queen's Birthday when Trooping the Colour. For some people this will be seen as an impressive statement and signal a collective display of steadiness and discipline (interestingly the colours were originally a signal for the rallying points on the battlefield). Equally, the gentle humility of one person to another can be signalled through a simple smile, conveying a message of kindness and support.

Signalling theory suggests that all evolutionary species send out signals as a form of information which influence outcomes. Therefore, as rational and conscious thinkers we have the capability to respond to the influences around us and the power to actively influence others every day.

- Every day we influence other people:
    - In what we say and how we say it
    - Through our language, slang, colloquialisms, jargon, dialect, pronunciation
    - In and how moods, emotions, feelings are expressed
    - In what we do and how we do it
    - In our manners and the consideration, we demonstrate to others
    - By giving advice (which may of course, sometimes be unsolicited!)
    - In our interest in things
    - In our dislike of things
    - In how we present ourselves

- ❖ Because of levels of personal hygiene
- ❖ Because of our body language
- ❖ Through our purchasing choices
- ❖ Through our lifestyle choices

- ♦ There are many reasons why we might influence other people on a day-to-day basis. For example, to:
    - ❖ Make a good first impression
    - ❖ Create a desired impression
    - ❖ Impress a new partner
    - ❖ Do well at an interview
    - ❖ Be approved of or even liked
    - ❖ Get our own way. For example, to sway choices such as going to a preferred restaurant, café, trip to the cinema, a day out or a holiday.
    - ❖ Get things done

- Inspire
- Motivate
- Get someone to act in their own best interests (as we see it)
- Teach children and others how to behave
- Sell a product or service
- Get a good price when negotiating a sale
- Promote an idea
- Sell a cause
- Raise money for charity
- Set standards

♦ Some examples of who you might influence:
- Family members
- Friends
- Social and other groups

- Club members
- Employers
- Line management
- Peers at work
- Associates
- People with whom you have something in common
- People with whom you come into contact who are not in your normal circle or with whom you may not have immediately obvious common interests
- Business groups and networks
- Neighbours
- Service providers
- The local and wider community
- Connections through social media

Part One.
Your Capacity to Influence

Recognising that we are all actors in an on-going drama

> *"All the world's a stage..."*

William Shakespeare

Psychologist Erving Goffman identified the dramaturgical nature of everyday interactions. In other words, we take part in a performance where social behaviour is a set of scripts in which we each have a role. Indeed, our language is littered with metaphors, advice and euphemisms illustrating the theatrical nature of the everyday performance:

- *'All the world's a stage and all the men and women merely players'*
- *'Making a drama out of a crises'*
- *'Don't worry about her, she's just a drama queen'*
- *'Give them the red-carpet treatment'*
- *'I'm struggling to get my lines straight'*
- *'Waiting in the wings'*
- *'The roar of the crowd'*
- *'Always leave them wanting more'*
- *'There's no dress rehearsal'*
- *'Taking the final bow'*

Our interactions often follow a pattern and a set of largely unwritten rules usually understood by everyone taking part. For example, an individual usually knows that when someone they are loosely acquainted with passes the time of day by saying *'How are you?'* that it is not an invitation to off load woes and worries. Or when buying a burger in most fast food chains that you do not ask to be seated and for someone to bring you the menu.

- We coordinate and dovetail our behaviour and language to be appropriate in many different environments including, for example:
    - At a wedding, christening and funeral
    - At a job interview
    - First day at work

- In meetings
- At a retirement party
- On a first date
- Living together, when a partner arrives home
- A visit to the theatre or a concert
- At a restaurant
- Small talk at a party or with new acquaintances
- In a shop
- On the school run - at the school gate
- At an auction
- Taking a vehicle to a garage for repair or sale
- A visit to the Doctors or Dentist
- At an airport or train station
- In a hotel
- On a beach

- In private

• Daily **we act** and **perform** to the **role** that we find ourselves in. This everyday behaviour tells us that we have the capacity to learn, adapt and influence. For example, we may adopt different personae such as:
  - Daughter / Son
  - Parent / Carer
  - Grandparent
  - Aunt / Uncle
  - Wife / Husband / Partner
  - Boyfriend / Girlfriend
  - Neighbour
  - Shopper / Supplier / Customer
  - Job role
  - Work colleague
  - Line Manager
  - Leader / Follower

- ❖ Business Associate
- ❖ Teacher / Pupil
- ❖ Doctor / Nurse / Patient
- ❖ Sportsperson
- ❖ Coach
- ❖ Mentor
- ❖ Close friend

♦ We can choose the behaviours, mantle and props that support our performance and have an opportunity to act and define our identity. This in turn provides a guide to others and enables them to act and coordinate their own performance. Some of the ways in which we convey impressions through the use of props etc:

- ❖ How we dress, including the fashion trends we choose to follow or ignore

- ❖ The quality and cut of fabrics and shoes
- ❖ Wearing designer labels
- ❖ How you wear your clothes. For example, ill-fitting, 'loud' ties, showing cleavage, open neck shirt or a shirt and tie, bright colours or muted tones
- ❖ How you maintain clothes and other possessions: Spick and span or dirty and dishevelled
- ❖ Accessories and accoutrements. For example, brand and model of mobile phone, brand and model of watch, make of eyewear, make of pen, the label on handbags or quality of luggage
- ❖ Jewellery
- ❖ Insignia: Badges, lapel pins, tie pins,

patterns woven into ties and clothes
- ❖ Uniforms
- ❖ Professional attire/costume such as that of the Judiciary
- ❖ Sports kit
- ❖ Body art
- ❖ Appearance and cleanliness. For example, hairstyle, makeup, perfume, body odour, level of grooming, 'manscaping'
- ❖ The places we choose to shop and the contents of shopping baskets
- ❖ The places where we choose to eat out, choose to visit for holidays etc.
- ❖ Our choice of leisure activities
- ❖ Our home and style
- ❖ The vehicle we use / car we drive
- ❖ In the work environment: Type and height of chair, size of desk,

entitlement to a car parking space

- Some of the ways in which we can choose to convey impressions with our behaviour:
    - The way you say something including speech, dialect and the use of professional terminology
    - Voice: shrill, deep, clear or muffled
    - Level of attentiveness
    - Level of kindness
    - Level of productivity
    - Level of engagement
    - Enthusiasm (or not) shown for things
    - Level of competitiveness
    - How we convey our feelings of confidence
    - How we either react or respond to matters

- ❖ Being secretive
- ❖ Being supportive
- ❖ Level of trustworthiness
- ❖ Level of discretion
- ❖ Gestures
- ❖ Open or closed body language. For example, posture that is bowed and tired or posture that is upright and vigorous etc.

- Sometimes other people will try to take the **role of Director** and attempt to impose an identity upon you. This phenomenon is called **Altercasting**. The advertising media is adept at the role of casting the audience into a role for the purpose of selling products. So, for example, people are steered by the direction of the advertiser to cast themselves into an identity that must be satisfied by making particular purchases or choices. At a more personal level examples of altercasting include:

- ❖ An overbearing person causing someone to feel helpless
- ❖ A bullying person causing someone to become submissive
- ❖ A needy person or group causing someone to take on too much responsibility

- ♦ It is also worth noting that there are of course occasions when others, including both the **audience** and other **actors** fail to understand their part, are out of step or resistant to roles either imposed or expected. This can occur for example when:
    - ❖ A person is perhaps under the influence of drink and drugs

- ❖ Someone is distracted
- ❖ An individual is under stress
- ❖ There are low levels of empathy
- ❖ There are low levels of understanding
- ❖ When someone has sociopathic tendencies

♦ The idea of taking roles and playing parts is perfectly illustrated in George Bernard Shaw's, Pygmalion and is captured in many big-name movies including:
   - ❖ My Fair Lady (the musical based on Pygmalion)
   - ❖ I Was Monty's Double
   - ❖ Tootsie
   - ❖ Working Girl
   - ❖ Pretty Woman

> "Clothes make a man. Naked people have little or no influence on society."

Mark Twain

'Case in Point'
Examples

There are many people who have famously understood their performance in creating and conveying impressions to have the desired effect:

The Suffragettes

The Suffragettes wore the combined colours of purple, white and green. Their distinct sashes and clothes were intended to convey a neat and well organised way of dressing. It was also believed by Emmeline Pankhurst that using fashion would counter the stereotypically views about suffragettes which had been promulgated at the time. Instead, adopting a different image would help when engaging in negotiations.

Billy Butlin / Megan Markle, Duchess of Sussex

It is said that when Billy Butlin was seeking to gain finance to fund his business ventures, he wanted to convey an impression of confidence and success. Despite having little money, he hired a Rolls Royce in which to turn up to an audience with potential backers as he was aware, they would be watching him when he arrived at the chosen venue for the meeting. He anticipated that the backers would see him from their viewpoint at the window!

Prior to her marriage to Prince Harry, it was widely reported by the press that Megan Markle had been so hard up during the time when she was auditioning for work that she was unable to afford repairs for her dilapidated 'hand-me-down' car. She was unable to open the front doors and so to avoid being seen clambering into the vehicle, would park in the furthest point at the back of the car park.

Mahatma Gandhi

As a Barrister Gandhi wore expensive European attire in an attempt to fit in with others. He later famously made a conscious decision and public statement when he stepped out in a Dhoti to signify his solidarity with the suffering of humanity.

Margaret Thatcher

Margaret Thatcher adapted her performance in a number of different ways. For example, she was coached to lower her voice; at the time it was considered too high and shrill. In addition, she understood and stated that *'I have to be in my best clothes seven days a week.'*

She also recognised the dramaturgical effects when she sought to appeal to a section of the electorate by identifying with the stereotyped 'common-sense housewife'. Thatcher notably presented herself as sweeping the front step while journalists gathered outside and was famous for carrying 'sensible' handbags.

Winston Churchill

Winston Churchill didn't have an overwhelmingly physical presence but the props he chose added to making him highly recognisable. His props such as wearing a bow tie, tall hats and using a cane presented a link with the past, which for some people may have provided a level of reassurance while other props such as his large cigars and his performance when delivering speeches famously added to his charisma.

George Orwell

George Orwell was acutely aware of the power of performance when he described an incident in India. He recounted how he believed himself to be an actor but felt like a puppet when he killed an Elephant to avoid looking like a fool in front of an expectant crowd.

Part Two.
Varieties of Influence

A summary of positive influencing skills

> *"Blessed is the influence of one true loving human soul on another."*

George Eliot

The benefits of positive influencing:

- You are likely to generate good will
- You can produce an effect without any apparent force
- If seeking to get things done through others:
    - *'One volunteer is better than ten pressed men'* (or women)
    - Gives people ownership of what they are doing
    - Self-esteem is kept intact if people feel they are doing something on a voluntary basis
    - Many people are simply not prepared to just do as they are told

- In general, positive influence can be achieved by being self-aware, alert and goal orientated:

- ❖ Understand people and *'what makes them tick'*
- ❖ Demonstrate understanding of other people
- ❖ Make informed decisions
- ❖ Provide information
- ❖ Gain support and commitment by seeking to find mutual gain

- ♦ Demonstrate strength of character and ethical behaviour that inspires others. For example:
    - ❖ Understand conditions, cause, effect and consequences
    - ❖ Recognise the significance of intentions and actions
    - ❖ Demonstrate trust and reliability by keeping commitments and holding to promises

- ❖ Where assurances have been given or expectations have been raised, ensure that you fulfil obligations
- ❖ Show loyalty to others
- ❖ Appreciate the right that people have to privacy
- ❖ Adhere to codes and standards of behaviour

"We never know which lives we influence, or when or why."

Stephen King

Part Two.
Varieties of Influence

Power

> *"What I believe is always true about power is that power always reveals."*

Robert Caro

There are occasions when influence is exerted due to the possession of different types of power.

- Power that arises from associations and connections between people:
    - Within personal relationships. For example, emotional or financial power
    - In the workplace. For example, new employee/established employee, manager/subordinate
    - Generational power
    - Bully/victim
    - Perceived social standing
    - Levels of wealth
    - Levels of dependency. For example, you have something such as knowledge or resources, that other people want
    - Expert/novice

- Power may arise because it has been bestowed and automatically recognised due to a person's position or by dint of tradition or agreed authority or role. For example:
    - Head of State
    - Religious leaders
    - Lineage
    - Job Role
    - Public Sector functions such as Police or the Armed Forces (as representatives of the law and the state)
    - The Nominated Officer coordinating incidents relating to health and safety
    - Politicians
    - Union Leaders
    - Employer/Employee

- Doctor/Patient
- Teacher/Student

♦ Power underwritten by knowledge, innovation, charisma and personal standing. For example:
- Gurus
- Innovators
- Role Models
- 'Disruptors' who may be forward thinking
- Leading authorities in the world of commerce, science, the arts etc.
- Ideologists
- People who possess ideas that reach into hearts and minds
- Cult leaders
- People for whom their time has come

- Famous people in the public eye
- Celebrity/social media personalities

* The benefits of having power to create effects:
  - In a crises power can exert calm and control
  - Power that has been bestowed positively as a consequence of tradition and authority means that people understand their role so providing respect, continuity and stability
  - The symbolism and power built into rules, regulations, policies etc. can eliminate chaos while bringing order and progress
  - Power can challenge the status quo
  - Power can bring about change

- ❖ Power can get things done

On the other hand, the use of power alone can -

- ♦ Lead others to:

    - ❖ Be resentful
    - ❖ Perhaps sabotage the perceived imposition of ideas, briefings and recommendations
    - ❖ Take an entrenched position
    - ❖ Behave half-heartedly
    - ❖ Absolve personal responsibility
    - ❖ Experience simmering discontent

- ♦ Lead the person with the perceived power to:

    - ❖ Abuse that power
    - ❖ Become intoxicated with excessive confidence and self-belief leaving them closed to the advice or

judgement of others
- ❖ Develop an inflated sense of entitlement
- ❖ Take reckless or ill-advised decisions and actions
- ❖ Feel enormous pressure to achieve
- ❖ Feel depleted
- ❖ Become isolated

- ♦ Create problems for relationships, groups, organisations and other structures:
  - ❖ People bestowed with power are not always *'up to the job'*
  - ❖ There may be indifference demonstrated to the checks and balances normally prudently applied to decision making and accountability
  - ❖ Risk management is disregarded

- ❖ Can spawn a '*Yes*' culture
- ❖ Can suppress innovation and enthusiasm
- ❖ May demoralise

Even if you have not been conferred with power, you still hold it in your hands, for you have the power to:

- ♦ Influence outcomes by using your right to vote
- ♦ Stand for public office
- ♦ Decide for yourself what you believe
- ♦ Ask questions, challenge assertions, beliefs and ideology
- ♦ Decide who you associate or align with
- ♦ Decide who or what you listen to
- ♦ Nurture future generations
- ♦ Make everyday decisions
- ♦ Make choices with respect to your personal behaviour and personal approach
- ♦ Inspire other people

"With great power comes great responsibility."

Voltaire

'Case in Point'
Examples

It is possible to reach the highest levels of influence without having first been conferred with formal power. Here is an eclectic sample of prominent influential individuals:

Anita Roddick, Founder of the Body Shop proved herself and built success by overcoming odds through **being innovative**, **hardworking** and **determined**.

Simon Cowell, Impresario and Promoter has created opportunities for other people around the world because he **understands the zeitgeist and what his audience wants.**

Tanni Grey-Thompson, as a Paralympian was **indefatigable**. She **did not give up** and became the best she could be.

Malala Yousafzai, Campaigner, was 'punished' for her activism but she has **overcome adversity**, **demonstrates conviction and energy** and **presents** great **moral authority**.

In addition, think of any number of:
- Great thinkers and experts from Newton to Einstein
- Designers and fashionistas from Coco Chanel to Vivien Westwood
- Individuals who have overcome diversity and provided inspiration from Douglas Bader to Simon Weston and Ben Parkinson
- Musicians, Artists, Writers and Broadcasters
- Pioneers and explorers

Part Two.
Varieties of Influence

Manipulation

"You campaign in poetry and govern in prose."

Mario Cuomo

Ethical influencing seeks to achieve a win/win outcome for all parties. On the other hand, some people adopt a mode of influence to seek control which is associated with an imbalance in relationships and manifests itself as manipulation. Manipulation can be demonstrated in a number of ways:

- Deliberate deceit and lies:
    - Blatant lying
    - Presenting falsified or misleading data and information
    - Sugar-coating the truth
    - Holding back, concealing or omitting information
    - Exaggeration
    - Propaganda
    - Being evasive
    - Concealing true position or intentions

- ❖ Exploiting a position of authority
- ❖ Plagiarism or passing others work off as one's own

- ♦ Playing psychological 'games' to mislead:
    - ❖ Feigning behaviours such as confusion, embarrassment or tears
    - ❖ Sham seduction or 'Love Bombing'
    - ❖ Keeping someone dangling and leaving them feeling uncertain
    - ❖ False flattery
    - ❖ Currying favour by fawning and ingratiating behaviours
    - ❖ Creating self-doubt in others
    - ❖ Stirring up anxiety, fear and anger
    - ❖ Creating a fog of confusion and then appearing to step in and sort things out
    - ❖ 'Gaslighting'

- ❖ Creating dependency
- ❖ Manipulating people from the shadows
- ❖ Playing at being a victim
- ❖ Beginning by asking for something small and then on the basis of agreement to that request asking for something else
- ❖ Putting people under pressure to decide, sign things off etc. when they are distracted. Perhaps when they are tired or in a hurry such as rushing out of the office to get home
- ❖ Wearing people down using abusive behaviours such as anger and intimidation through to 'the silent treatment' and sulking

- ♦ The reasons why people manipulate:

- ❖ They may not know any better – it is learned behaviour, or it is the way they have been treated and so they choose to behave like it too
- ❖ To gain approval
- ❖ To increase personal self-esteem
- ❖ Out of boredom
- ❖ Fear – they have backed themselves into a corner
- ❖ For the purpose of propaganda
- ❖ To gain power and control
- ❖ A lack of compassion
- ❖ A lack of morals
- ❖ Callous nature
- ❖ Criminality

In the short term, manipulation may yield results and gains but ultimately trust is lost. The person doing the manipulating will be exposed and discredited which in turn may leaving them isolated and damaged. Meanwhile, those who have been manipulated may feel let down, hurt and exploited. The manipulated person may alter their future behaviour; they might develop caution, scepticism or even dislike, anxiety and fear.

"For when the One Great Scorer comes to mark against your name, He writes – not that you won or lost - but how you played the game."

Grantland Rice

Part Two.
Varieties of Influence

Persuasion and proposition

During our everyday lives we navigate many examples of persuasion and proposition as these techniques are used to change behaviour, sell an idea, cause or product. Typically:

- Campaigns such as free support offered to stop smoking
- The use of fear: Conjuring anxiety that if you don't buy into something or do something you will have problems. For example, services such as insurance for white goods. At an individualist level, Benefit Claimants told that allowances will be withdrawn if they don't comply with regulations
- Advertising techniques which prompt you into measuring yourself against others by suggesting that if you follow a particular course of action or buy certain products you could be like someone with whom you

would wish to be associated, be it one of 'the beautiful people', an admired sports hero or celebrity
- Politicians or advertisers using the appeal of endorsements or the views of common sense, 'authentic' ordinary plain-speaking people
- Comparing the number of products, you can buy from one supermarket with another
- BOGOF 'Buy one get one free' offers
- The price being held for a limited period
- The use of the 'Carrot or Stick' to motivate someone to do something
- The 'If/Then' methodology used during negotiations (Preparing to give something up on the basis of getting something in return)
- Finally, who hasn't heard the appeal of a

child exclaiming that *'everybody else is doing it'*

The techniques shown can be summed up as using:

- Inducements or incentives. For example, bonuses or employee incentive schemes. The promise of awards, perks, or recognition
- Rewards such as praise
- Bribery – promises to provide something of benefit which may be desired or seen as a reward. However, sometimes an offer may present a moral dilemma particularly when harm to the person is involved
- Persuasion by the use of associations.
- Putting someone under pressure to decide *('Make your mind up because I can't wait for ever…')*
- Appeals to act *('You scratch my back, I'll scratch yours)*

- Arguments for and against

There can be a fine line between influencing someone using a persuasive approach and manipulation. For example, individuals might feel that they have been tricked by inducements or duped by the techniques of a 'snake oil salesman' who has knowingly exploited their trust by defrauding them. Bribery may operate at a simple level such as a parent offering sweets at the supermarket to control an unruly toddler. On the other hand, bribery can lead to corruption and may create a destructive power dynamic with lasting repercussions. With respect to arguments and appeals, an individual may feel that they are left with no choice particularly if they are faced with a question or predicament presented as a **'false dilemma fallacy'.** In this case phrases similar to those as *'You're either with us, or against us'* manipulate by forcing a choice, or imposing an alternative option which is at the polar opposite of the spectrum. This creates a false dichotomy and leaves a person in a position where they are unable to explore or express other alternatives or possibilities. Furthermore, dependent upon circumstances, they can be left feeling under pressure, unsure, vulnerable and isolated.

- The key to ethical influencing when using persuasion or proposition is that:
    - Individuals should be provided with facts that they can then work with
    - Individuals should feel that they have a reasonable choice
    - Integrity should be applied
    - Individuals should have their self-esteem left in-tact

Part Three. Sphere/Circle of Influence

> *"In a gentle way you can shake the world."*

Mahatma Gandhi

Your sphere/circle of influence

The notion of a circle or a sphere of influence is a metaphor used to illustrate the scope of your influence.

- There are two different aspects with respect to your sphere/circle of influence:
    - **The focus of your influence**. In other words, recognising **the issues and matters over which you have influence**
    - The **extent or reach of your influence**. This may be with individuals, groups of people, teams, organisations etc.

Your focus of influence

- Your focus of influence means that you are putting your energy into those things over which you can have confidence and control

The extent or reach of your influence

The extent or reach of your personal influence recognises those with whom you have greater or lesser influence.

- Personal influence:
    - In using the metaphor of a sphere or circle of influence we can consider ourselves in the middle of a circle. Those with whom we have most influence are closest to the centre of the circle. Often these are people with whom we share close ties or areas of commonality. Typically, our level of personal influence is considered to grow weaker further from the centre, a little bit like throwing a pebble into water and seeing the ripples travel outwards

- Sphere of influence as a consequence of formal power:
    - Power as a result of tradition, authority or conferred by position automatically enhances the extent or reach of your personal influence

> *"There is so much we can do to render service, to make a difference in the world - no matter how large or small our circle of influence."*

Stephen Covey

Part Three.
Expanding your Personal Influence

> *"I am only one, but still I am one. I cannot do everything, but still I can do something. And because I cannot do everything, I will not refuse to do the something I can do."*

Edward Everett Hale

Your reach and the extent of your influence can be achieved in different ways.

- First, develop self-awareness and engage in personal self-management:
    - Appreciate that your own mental control and mental outlook provide the key to unlocking success
    - Balance the information you receive and increase your knowledge and skills with respect to decision making
    - Read widely to spot, follow and create trends
    - The right daily routines and habits are important to wellbeing and being at your best. For example, rather than allowing things to build up and potentially cause problems, ensure you keep doing the 'little

things' and don't 'brush things under the carpet'
- ❖ Be aware of how others see you
- ❖ Be aware of how you are portrayed
- ❖ Appreciate your capacity to 're-brand'
- ❖ Improve your performance. However, be mindful that just keeping your head down is not enough (indeed you could find yourself being exploited)
- ❖ Be flexible about adapting your behaviour and approach
- ❖ Learn how to act: Visualise and practice in your head exchanges with others, making presentations etc.
- ❖ Understand that sometimes the choice to 'play the game' may be

necessary. For example, if you are working with customers and need to or are seeking to influence behaviour you may need to do this by altering perceptions
- ❖ Be the best version of you

- ♦ Identify your current extent or your reach of influence
  - ❖ Identify the areas where your influence is weak
  - ❖ Identify who, what, where you can influence
  - ❖ Decide where your influence is best needed
  - ❖ Develop strategy and plans to broaden your influence
  - ❖ Be prepared to review and alter initial aims

- ❖ Take incremental steps to achieve ultimate goals

- ◆ Raise your profile by:
  - ❖ Attending meetings
  - ❖ Being visible at meetings. For example, think about where you seat yourself at the table in meetings and the contribution that you make
  - ❖ Having one-to-one meetings
  - ❖ Attending social functions
  - ❖ Attending conferences
  - ❖ Attending networking events and work to be known as able to contribute
  - ❖ Considering the type of network etc that best serves your purpose: A practitioner network where professionals share similar

interests, an ideological group, power networks which build influential relationships or networks designed to provide support

❖ Being mindful when attending new networks to create open conversations by asking people questions such as "Why they are there?" While at the same time be thoughtful about how, when and what information you convey.

❖ Positioning yourself in the centre of the group when photographs are being taken

❖ Engaging in workplace team activities, retreats and weekend events

❖ Making presentations

- ❖ Using social media
- ❖ Appearing on platforms such as TV, Radio and the Internet
- ❖ Writing in newspapers, journals, annual reports etc.
- ❖ Making yourself indispensable, the 'go to' resource
- ❖ Attaching yourself to a cause
- ❖ Engaging in kindly, charitable and philanthropic works

- ♦ Relationships:
  - ❖ Use 'political skills' by identifying those people who are in powerful positions (which may not be the obvious person). Gently and patiently get known until you are accepted
  - ❖ Notice and align with the

behaviours, attitudes and values that are acceptable to others
- ❖ Participate in the rituals and norms that bind people together
- ❖ Grow and strengthen connections such as with people who provide the bridge from one group to another
- ❖ Develop new relationships by reaching out to those who are 'weak ties'. These are wide ranging acquaintances who in some cases you may not even meet such as connections through social media
- ❖ Associate and align with those with whom you can develop a ground swell of support
- ❖ Create alliances
- ❖ Associate or work with 'social

networkers' as these people are likely to 'spread the word'
- ❖ Ensure your ideas, proposals, innovations reach 'early adopters'. These being either individuals or organisations who open to the new and are motivated to try and champion things that are fresh and different and are in a position to promote suggestions
- ❖ Make sure you're talking to the right people; Analyse stakeholders and identify decision makers and levels of decision making
- ❖ Maintain regular contact with people

- ♦ Be genuinely open to the influence of others:

- ❖ Ask questions
- ❖ Show attention and actively listen
- ❖ Act on ideas and information
- ❖ Give credit where it is due

♦ Finally, understand that *'being in the right place at the right time'* is not always by dint of luck but **requires effort, persistence and determination**

"Success always demands greater effort."

Winston Churchill

Part Four.
Influencing Techniques

Choosing to be assertive:
The alternative options

To the Point

> *"A man is what he thinks about all day long."*

Ralph Waldo Emmerson

Effective Behaviour – Choosing to be Assertive

Personal effectiveness and influencing is about selecting appropriate behaviour which, in most cases is about choosing to be assertive. However, it is also worth noting that behaviour and approach may necessarily be modified and determined by different situations, by the company of different people and shaped by different cultures and environments.

Assertiveness embraces an attitude and behaviour that is generally presented as being on a continuum between two polarities, namely passivity and aggression with different shades of functioning located across the whole. Where appropriate, an assertive person may choose to adopt a passive or aggressive approach as demanded by the situation. For example, to cool a situation, to avoid escalating uncontrollable anger in others, in cases of passive resistance or in matters of urgency. On the other hand, choosing to act in a passive or aggressive way as the norm is likely to be inappropriate and has far reaching consequences for all. Therefore, in understanding assertion it is useful to first discuss passive and aggressive behaviour.

An overview of typically passive characteristics

Passive behaviour can be identified where instinctive behaviour pivots around avoidance or accommodating others. The passive person is *'acted upon, rather than acting'* at the expense of personal rights, viewpoints and desires.

- The mark of passive behaviour:
    - Deferential
    - Compliant
    - Often the one to be lumbered with the jobs that no one else wants to do

- Timid
- Indecisive and hesitant
- Difficulty in expressing or doesn't come right out with wants, needs and feelings, *'Beats about the bush'*
- Ignores, avoids, fears or mitigates disagreements and conflict when it might better be confronted
- Allows personal beliefs and boundaries to be overridden
- Goes along with the crowd, frequently subsuming own wants
- When faced with problems, does nothing in the hope they will go away
- Always aiming to please
- Overly apologetic
- Keeps quiet when feeling unfairly treated, *'Suffers in silence'*

- ❖ Resigned to giving in *'Anything for a quiet life'*

How passive behaviour may influence others

- ♦ Initially:
    - ❖ Seen as being nice
    - ❖ Creates a perception of being a giving person and so in turn elicit a belief that they are loving and agreeable
    - ❖ Generate kindness from others
    - ❖ Creates sympathy
    - ❖ Lead others to act as the 'rescuer'
    - ❖ Others may welcome that someone is amenable or isn't going to *'create waves'*
    - ❖ Is seen as open to persuasion
    - ❖ Creates a lead in for manipulators and aggressors

- Longer term:
  - Produces pity
  - Produces irritation as passive individuals may be seen as people *'who can't help themselves'*
  - Resentment at their failure to take personal responsibility
  - Initiatives aren't taken
  - Problems are not addressed
  - Decisions are deferred or avoided
  - Causes a lack of respect
  - Can create an unhealthy addictive co-dependent victim dynamic
  - Becomes a 'doormat'

An overview of typically aggressive characteristics

An aggressive person typically displays behaviour and approach which is usually at the expense of the rights of others. There is often a desire to win at any cost and an inclination for power over other people. Freud ultimately regarded aggression as *'a projection of the death impulse'*.

- The features of aggressive behaviour:
  - An approach whereby, *'No one is going to get the better of me'*. *'Attack is the best form of defence'*. *'Doesn't suffer fools gladly'*
  - Overbearing
  - Antagonistic
  - Frequently staring people down
  - Imposes their solutions
  - Forcing others to play their way by trying to control those around them
  - Arrogant
  - One-upmanship
  - Threatening

- ❖ Uses coercion
- ❖ Unable to accept feedback or difference of opinion
- ❖ Blunt to the point of rudeness and/or being offensive, *'Calls a spade a spade'*
- ❖ Always ready to complain
- ❖ Sarcastic
- ❖ Difficulty in controlling anger and temper
- ❖ Impatient
- ❖ Does not listen

How aggressive behaviour may influence others

- ♦ Initially:
    - ❖ Elicit admiration for being tough
    - ❖ Grateful that someone is prepared to take charge
    - ❖ Perhaps generates admiration for

getting things done

- Longer term:
  - Others may feel humiliated and resentful
  - Others may feel hurt
  - Others may feel angry
  - Stifles initiative
  - Sucks the energy out of individuals or on getting things done
  - Suppresses cooperation and so people withhold information or reduce contact
  - Causes people to 'go underground' or do things behind the aggressors back
  - Elicits retaliation
  - Creates conflict
  - Like the passive person, the

aggressive individual leaves themselves as vulnerable to a manipulative person who may see opportunities to steer the aggressor's behaviour for their own ends

❖ Others may ignore and avoid the aggressive individual, leaving them isolated and lonely

An overview of typically passive/aggressive characteristics

Aggressive/passive behaviour has roots in the belief that *'I can't win but I'm not going to lose'*

- Passive/aggressive behaviour can be identified as follows:
    - ❖ Disengaged
    - ❖ Uncooperative
    - ❖ Sullen

- Vengeful
- Devious
- Appearing to play the *'good guy'*
- Vague
- Artificially self-effacing
- Holding onto simmering resentments
- Manipulative
- Snide remarks and asides
- Saying one thing while meaning another
- Expert in creating rumour and gossip
- Agreeing or arranging to do something and having no intention of doing it or purposefully delaying doing it or completing activities in an unsatisfactory fashion
- Doesn't complete anything

- ❖ Taking pleasure in the anxiety of others when dealing with problems
- ❖ Prevents others from experiencing success or joy

How passive/aggressive behaviour may influence others

- ♦ Initially:
  - ❖ Grateful that on the surface problems appear to be solved

- ♦ Longer term:
  - ❖ Respect is lost
  - ❖ People may not trust the passive/aggressive person
  - ❖ Individuals may reduce or withdraw contact
  - ❖ Little is achieved

To the Point

Part Four. Influencing Techniques

Choosing to be assertive: Effective behaviour

"Setting an example is not the main means of influencing others, it is the only means."

Albert Einstein

Choosing to be Assertive. Effective Behaviour

Assertiveness is behaviour built upon a positive self-concept, self-confidence, self-control and self-determination combined with a philosophy of personal responsibility. It is the ability to say what you want, think and/or feel while being aware of the rights of others and leaving the self-esteem of people intact.

Ideally an assertive individual looks to achieve a win/win outcome, recognising that *'I'm okay, you're okay'*. However, assertiveness is an approach that also understands the need to be a realist and to take a pragmatic approach. Therefore, where it is logical and makes sense, an assertive person is prepared to back down, compromise, trade-off or fight. The assertive person can be tough and effective in the heat of conflict or during periods of discord, being able to address matters directly but also recognising when it might be more successful to choose alternative options such as helping people to save face or where the place, time and energy needed to resolve problems is simply not right.

An overview of typically assertive characteristics

- Perspective:
    - Self-aware: Understanding one's personal story and recognises how this may affect emotions
    - Self-acceptance: Feeling okay about the self, not intimidated or driven by the negative put-downs or drivers of other people
    - Able to cope with life's setbacks
    - An assertive person appreciates their personal gifts, be it knowledge, skills, the wonder of their own body, health and

capabilities
- ❖ Recognises the abundance of life rather than having a scarcity mentality which can lead to competition and strife: An assertive person sees what is possible
- ❖ Acts in the faith that there is something that each party within an interaction can at least find to admire in each other
- ❖ Guided by principles, values and goals
- ❖ Sets personal boundaries and respects the personal boundaries of others
- ❖ Understands that they have rights as a human and that others have those same rights too
- ❖ Recognises where lessons can be

learned
- ❖ Keeps knowledge and skills up to date
- ❖ Recognises that they have the power to create opportunities
- ❖ Takes ownership for their fundamental sense of self-esteem
- ❖ Understands the need to maintain and put into place strategies for personal wellbeing

- ♦ Features:
    - ❖ Confident
    - ❖ Demonstrates confidence in behaviour, actions and words
    - ❖ Balanced
    - ❖ Calm
    - ❖ Mindful
    - ❖ Even-tempered

- ❖ Able to control personal impulses and emotions
- ❖ Doesn't easily 'rise to the bait'
- ❖ Doesn't repress emotions but positively acts and uses emotions or overcomes them
- ❖ Able to take a position beyond the immediate moment and consider longer term consequences by reflecting and asking questions such as: *'Will I regret saying this in the future?' 'What will be the long-term effect upon this relationship if I take this approach?'*
- ❖ Productively uses an understanding of emotions to clarify and explain the effects of negative behaviour
- ❖ Rational

- ❖ Responds instead of reacting
- ❖ Open-minded
- ❖ Non-judgemental
- ❖ Accepts that mistakes happen
- ❖ Recognise that they are equal to others and treats others as equals
- ❖ Appreciates the effective attributes of others
- ❖ Expresses acceptance, respect, appreciation and praise for others
- ❖ Flexible, able to cope with ambiguity and change
- ❖ Problem solving approach
- ❖ Maintains a focus on issues rather than personalising matters
- ❖ Collaborative
- ❖ Able to jointly work through problems
- ❖ Uses questions to find out the

views, opinions, needs, wants and feelings of others
- ❖ An active listener
- ❖ Empathetic
- ❖ Makes a distinction between facts and opinions
- ❖ Observant to the prevailing mood of the room
- ❖ Feels confident in being able to ask for help or information
- ❖ Gives suggestions
- ❖ Trustworthy
- ❖ Positive and constructive
- ❖ Chooses to be assertive as appropriate to the situation

How assertive behaviour influences others

- ♦ Initially:
    - ❖ Those individuals who are prone to

being passive or aggressive or people who are often in the company of passive or aggressive individuals may initially feel awkward or unsettled by an assertive person
- ❖ Could be considered to be boring and lacking in passion
- ❖ Might be seen as aloof

- ♦ Short term to longer term:
    - ❖ Relationships are improved
    - ❖ People will enjoy interacting and having the company of the assertive individual
    - ❖ Cooperation and achievement is realised
    - ❖ Ideas are generated
    - ❖ Mutual respect is developed

- ❖ Trust is high
- ❖ Commitment is gained
- ❖ Relationships are maintained and may be strengthened
- ❖ Increases the chance of high quality end results
- ❖ Assertive behaviour may be fostered in others

Conversely
- ❖ For those individuals who enjoy a bit of drama, the assertive person may be someone to be goaded into losing their cool
- ❖ May provoke jealousy in some

Assertive behaviours

- ♦ Non-verbal communication:
    - ❖ Relaxed and steady facial expression

- Smiles take place when happy or pleased, not as an aggressive jeering or sly behaviour
- Eye contact is maintained without trying to stare down
- When listening, gives people undivided attention
- Posture is open with the body and head upright
- Walks with purpose and energy
- Hand motions are open with a measured pace
- Shakes hands powerfully
- Dress and general appearance is appropriate and at it's best

- Para-verbal communication: Choice and tone of words:
  - Speech is articulate and smooth,

    making for easy listening
- ❖ A pace that is steady and even
- ❖ Middle to lower pitch of voice which is not too loud or too quiet
- ❖ Sincere

- ◆ Verbal communication:
    - ❖ At its basic level assertive communication follows **a three-step approach**: First, an assertive person will listen, show that they hear and understand. Secondly, the assertive individual says what they want, think or feel. Finally, after questioning and listening, they will say what they want to happen
    - ❖ If necessary, an assertive person ensures their message is heard by **reiterating the main points**. This

technique recognises that sometimes other people may be preoccupied with their own interests and their attention may be reduced. Therefore, without giving someone a dressing down or criticising them for not listening, the assertive person will calmly repeat key words and restate the essential core of the message until they are confident it has been noted and retained

- ❖ The assertive person understands that sometimes when people are behaving aggressively, they may be looking for an argument or seeking disagreement. With this in mind, as appropriate, rather than engage in negativity, the assertive person will look to '**take the heat out of the situation'** by responding to the aggressive person in a way that '**takes the wind out of their sails'.** To do this the assertive person listens to what is being said (or shouted!) and comes back with a statement which is likely to be at odds with the anticipated response. The assertive person does not agree with the arguments but uses the word *'Yes'* and agrees that they can see that the aggressor might believe something, feel something etc. In doing this the assertive person slows things down and alters the course of a tricky situation

❖ In building solid relationships, the assertive person recognises that simmering emotions and resentments are detrimental to wellbeing. Therefore, there may be occasions when **addressing the negative impact of the behaviour of another person** needs to be confronted and when the feelings such behaviour arouses are best expressed. (It is worth noting that not all behaviour is intentional, and some people may not be aware of the impact of their behaviour on others). The approach to this situation is to be constructive and proportionate. To do this the assertive person states what they have observed and without criticising simply expresses the impact that the behaviour has upon them, the feelings that it arouses in them and the effect it has upon getting things done. This then opens up a dialogue for a positive plan of action for moving forward

- ❖ **Compromise:** An assertive person knows that everyone sometimes has to engage in making concessions and find a practical solution to problems that is reasonably acceptable to all. An assertive approach to compromise is about developing a solution whereby each party is asked to move towards the middle ground by considering and building a third option formulated from initial positions namely: your solution, my solution and our solution

> *"We have two ears and one mouth so that we can listen twice as much as we speak."*

Epictetus

Part Four.
Influencing Techniques

Being a great listener

"Wise men speak because they have something to say; Fools because they have to say something."

Plato

The power of listening

The value of listening as an influencing tool is underpinned when we consider that advertising companies spend millions on listening to what consumers want. Leadership skills training encourages individuals to be curious, to listen and to be open to finding out what is going on and why. And as we have seen listening is a key element of being assertive.

- The benefits of listening:
    - Improves relationships
    - Improves understanding (even if there is no agreement)
    - Aids problem solving and decision making
    - In some circumstances, by listening to people it will help them to lose any defensiveness

Listening can be hindered for any number of reasons:

- Physical barriers:
    - Noise or other distractions
    - An uncomfortable or untidy environment
    - The actual physical distance between the talker and the listener

- Social and psychological barriers:
    - First impressions
    - The emotional distance between the talker and the listener
    - Personal differences
    - Suddenly being lovestruck
    - Social values
    - Attitudes
    - Prejudging the content of communication and the person

delivering it
- ❖ Holding bias or stereotypes with respect to the person talking
- ❖ An inability to concentrate
- ❖ Tiredness
- ❖ Boredom
- ❖ Simply not interested in what is being said
- ❖ Over familiar with the speaker and so takes them for granted and fails to give 100% when listening
- ❖ Other things which divert attention as being more interesting either than what is being said or who is saying it
- ❖ Expecting the person doing the talking to be scintillating or interesting
- ❖ We can think faster than people can

talk and so sometimes we think ahead when others are speaking
- ❖ Anxiety concerning the content of the exchange
- ❖ Interruptions to the communication
- ❖ A desire to put our own point across

- ♦ Semantic barriers (the meaning of the words spoken):
    - ❖ Words can have more than one meaning
    - ❖ Some people find it difficult to put their thoughts and feelings into words
    - ❖ Some people have a limited vocabulary
    - ❖ The use of jargon
    - ❖ The way that things are said. For example, accent, emphasis, tone,

incomprehensible, muddled
- ❖ The use of emotive words, statements and declarations

- **Effective listening skills.**

  Listen with thoughtfulness:
  - ❖ Be mindful of the physical, social, psychological and semantic barriers
  - ❖ Make the choice to really focus and concentrate on what is being said
  - ❖ Recognise fact from fiction
  - ❖ Try to understand the talker's point of view
  - ❖ Spot ideas
  - ❖ Notice emerging themes
  - ❖ Observe the non-verbal signals such as the way things are being said, tone of voice, body language, facial expressions and the feelings being

conveyed. Sometimes you may need to ask yourself if what is being said is at odds/congruent with the emotions and behaviour being communicated?

- **Effective listening skills.**
  Show that you are/have been listening:
  - Use para language such as *'Ah ha'*
  - Use nonverbal communication. For example, maintain good eye contact and position yourself towards the person who is speaking
  - Ask relevant questions
  - Seek clarification or ask the talker to repeat what they have been saying
  - Paraphrase and summarise what you have heard
  - In certain situations you may need

to take notes. (N.B Dependent upon the situation, as a courtesy you should advise the speaker that you will be taking notes. In certain cases, you may need permission to take notes and to provide information about how the notes will be processed)

- **Effective listening skills.**
  Show respect to the talker:
  - ❖ When responding, be reflective by saying something like *'I can see this means a great deal to you …'*
  - ❖ Acknowledge ideas, opinions and viewpoints
  - ❖ Ensure you have fully understood before concluding and evaluating what has been said

To the Point

Part Four.
Influencing Techniques

Questioning

> *"You can tell whether a man is clever by his answers. You can tell whether a man is wise by his questions."*

Naquib Mahfouz

> I keep six honest serving men…
> (They taught me all I knew)
> Their names are **what** and **why** and **when**
> And **how** and **where** and **who**

The opening lines to Rudyard Kipling's poem about his inquisitive daughter provide a neat mnemonic about questioning. From an early age questioning as a tool provides untold value in building our knowledge and comprehension of the world around us and in terms of influencing, is usually a neat adjunct to listening.

- The purpose of questioning as an influencing tool:
    - As appropriate, to relax people and encourage them to talk
    - To understand other people; their frames of reference, what drives

- their behaviour and the views/position that they hold
- To find out what other people want and need
- To get below the surface
- To see life through the eyes of other people
- To achieve a 'meeting of minds'
- To enable an informed judgement rather than attempting to 'mind-read' or engage in a guessing game
- To avoid assumptions
- To collect information to make an objective assessment
- To pin people down with respect to decision making, getting on board with an issue, gaining commitment etc
- To show sensitivity and relevance

to people and avoid a blunderbuss approach when influencing outcomes
- ❖ To indicate interest and appreciation of other people
- ❖ To establish that what you have heard while listening, is correct
- ❖ To control an interaction

- ♦ Basic question types:
    - ❖ **Open questions.** These questions encourage people to talk. They are useful for gathering information and generally cannot be answered with a one-word reply. For example, *'What do you mean...?' 'Why is that?' 'How do you do that?' 'What did you learn from that?'*
    - ❖ **Closed questions** generally elicit a

yes or no response. They can be useful if you want to limit discussion. For example, *'Did you…?' 'Do you understand?'*

- ❖ **Specific/factual questions.** These questions drill down to facts and clarify particular points. For example, *'How many?' 'How long did it take?' 'When did that happen?' 'What systems did you use?'*
- ❖ **Comparative questions** enable you to make an evaluation. For example, *'How did the role differ from an earlier position?' 'How did the roles compare?'*

- Types of questions to be avoided:
    - ❖ **Multiple questions** can be very confusing for the person who is expected to answer; they may not

know which question to answer first or might even fail to recall all of the questions asked. For example, *'What was the best part about the role you used to have, what was your main responsibility and what didn't you like doing?'*

❖ **Leading questions** can put words into the mouth of the person who is answering. For example, *'You haven't got what I want have you?' 'You haven't done this have you?' 'You don't want to do that, do you?' 'Did that mean a lot of effort on your part?'*

❖ **Value loaded questions** implicitly communicate an expression of worth or bias. For example, *'So you only did…?' 'Why on earth did you do that?' 'Only come for a visit if you* *really want to; so, what do you want to do?'*

- Pitfalls to avoid when using questions:
    - Going straight into the heart of the matter (as you see it), as this may appear to be intrusive
    - Overcomplicating issues by asking too many questions
    - Trying to probe for something that just isn't there or of little importance to the person being questioned (People's values, attitudes and viewpoints may be different to your own)
    - Putting someone under pressure
    - Causing someone to become flustered with too many questions

Questions can be configured into a wide variety of

arrangements to meet different needs. So, if for example you are helping someone to explore a particular situation you might encourage them by asking questions arranged in a sequence to identify possibilities and alternatives, advantages and disadvantages and how ideas are to be taken forward. If you are conducting an interview you might use the 'funnel approach' to probe for information. If you are counselling, you are likely to use a sequence of non-directive questioning to help an individual to arrive at a solution to a personal problem.

- ♦ The sequence of questions typically used when seeking information as an influencing tool takes a three step approach. However, these steps can reach quite deeply into a person's beliefs and world view. Therefore, you should follow the sequence with care, listen and observe cues before deciding whether to move through each of the steps:

- ❖ **Facts.** These questions sit at the top of the sequence and are usually basic in nature and form the routine and ritualistic nature of most interaction. For example, *'When?' 'Where?' 'How? 'What do you do?' 'Have you been on holiday this year?' 'What's the problem?' 'Where does it hurt?'*

- ❖ **The meaning behind the facts.** Typically, you might use this type of question about a third of the time. For example, *'What do you think of x?' 'Do you like what you do?'* If the answer is yes, *'What is it about what you do that you enjoy?'* If the answer to the first question is no *'What is it about what you do that you dislike?' 'What did you like about your holiday?' 'How does it affect you emotionally?' 'How are you feeling?'*

❖ **The values that lie behind the facts**. This type of question is not usually used on a daily basis. For example, *'Why do you feel that?' 'Why is it important to you to do what you do?' 'Why was it of interest to you to go there for your holiday?'* Questions at this level may be considered to be somewhat intrusive within the normal routines of life and so should only be used when you are satisfied that a person is comfortable with the first two stages of the sequence. To illustrate this point, this is the level of questioning that you might hear when an intimate relationship is being formed and each of the partners seeks to know the other deeply.

'Case in Point'
Examples

On the 26th September 1960 the first televised United States Presidential Election Debate took place. The debate took place between Richard Nixon who was a seasoned politician serving as the incumbent Vice President and John Kennedy who was considered to be young and lacking in experience. The debate was a pivotal moment as it is believed that it changed the course of American (and quite possibly, world) history. With respect to influencing it had a powerful impact in terms of altering ideas about how people are judged.

Listening, Questions and Being Open to Influence

Before taking part in the debate Kennedy listened and took advice about appearing on television. He spent the whole weekend prior to the debate staying with his aides in a hotel where he couldn't be disturbed and where he spent hours practicing questions. Nixon did not.

The Dramaturgical Effect

Famously, Kennedy was noted for his healthy-looking tan which was enhanced by a touch of expertly applied stage make-up. On the other hand, Nixon refused stage make-up instead opting to use his own thick 'Pan-Stick' foundation in an attempt to mask a 5 o'clock' shadow (which, although when well-groomed today can be quite a fashion statement was considered at that time to be unkempt). In addition, as Nixon perspired and appeared under stress the Pan-Stick foundation began to melt away revealing an ashen complexion.

Nixon's ashen appearance was further exaggerated in his choice of light grey suit which caused him to appear to fade further into the background. Meanwhile, Kennedy was impeccably groomed, in a dark suit.

Assertiveness (including Body Language)

While preparing at the hotel, Kennedy had understood the need to maintain personal wellbeing and so had taken the opportunity for sleep and rest. At the same time Nixon had continued to push himself by staying on the campaign trail. This despite having recently recovered from a knee injury, a bout of flu and being generally low powered.

During the debate Kennedy appeared calm and confident, he stared straight into the camera and used his finger to emphasise key points. Nixon avoided direct eye contact and was described as appearing weak.

Nixon lost the debate and thereafter his campaign failed to recover. This episode emphasis that the *'medium is the message'*. In other words, how you connect with and influence people has as much to do with how you present yourself, how you look and sound as it does with the content. YOU are embedded within the message and in a world of first impressions, quick glimpses and where perceptions versus reality, no more so than now.

> *"It is not what you say, but how you say it."*

Unknown

Part Four.
Influencing Techniques

Building Rapport

> *"Friendship is born at the moment when one person says to another, What you too? I thought I was the only one."*

C.S. Lewis

Rapport within the context of influencing is about reaching people in such a way as to show and create agreement on the basis that you are like them or that you at least understand them. This in turn can generate loyalty, support for and acceptance of ideas, willingness to cooperate and feelings of harmony and unanimity.

The advantage of rapport is that when people feel understood it provides reassurance and reduces anxiety. In turn, effectiveness can be increased as the mood of individuals is altered.

Deep rapport can sometimes be observed in strong, close relationships where understanding is so great that meaning can be conveyed with nothing needing to be said at all. Accord is such that individuals are able to finish each other's sentences and body language is reflected as though seen through a looking glass.

The extent to which you implement the knowledge and skills of building rapport depends upon the level of the interaction and desired outcomes. In developing rapport, you are disclosing personal authenticity but be careful as this may open up areas of emotional vulnerability. For example, don't willy-nilly share your life or wear your heart on your sleeve. Be astute and be cautious about how you share ideas, for as discussed earlier there are some people who can be unpleasant and some that can be manipulative. Assess the extent of your self-disclosure and consider as necessary the need to maintain a professional distance.

How to build rapport

- After establishing the purpose of your communication, use questioning and listening to seek information and learn about other people:

- ❖ What are their viewpoints?
- ❖ What are they committed to?
- ❖ What do they feel is worth talking about?
- ❖ What do they like or dislike?
- ❖ What sort of interests do they have?
- ❖ Where do you share common ground?

♦ Communicate appropriate information about yourself:
  - ❖ Share your interests
  - ❖ Share your own thoughts
  - ❖ Express your personal concerns
  - ❖ Share your emotions
  - ❖ Share your own feelings

If you are presenting to an audience, when expressing emotions and feelings, either positive or feeling fed up or frustrated, imagine how you would sound if you were talking to someone close and then practice conveying the same level of passion with a larger group of people.

- Acknowledge where you share similarities:
    - Make known areas of common interests
    - Express shared values
    - Indicate shared feelings

- Help to put others at ease:
    - You may wish to show that you are alike by displaying signifiers which indicate common bonds such as group membership pins/badges
    - Whether with a large audience or one-to-one, create a convivial atmosphere. This may range from encouraging a social environment

or meeting somewhere relaxing, perhaps over a pleasant meal or coffee

- ❖ Give praise where is it due
- ❖ If in a professional environment use relevant professional terminology. Otherwise try to avoid jargon
- ❖ Ensure that there is consistency between your verbal and non-verbal language
- ❖ Use phrases and words which indicate shared experience, provide empathy, areas of commonality or signal joint action. For example, *'I had an experience like the one you're describing, I agree it was great fun'* *'Remember that time when we enjoyed x?'* *'We agreed last week that we would do x'*

- If acceptable and appropriate, provide small favours or gifts (but don't overdo things as recipients may feel overwhelmed or indebted). N.B You should also be minded that in the work environment, some individuals may be under obligation to either refuse or put on the record favours or gifts as part of organisational policy and procedure in order to mitigate against fraud and corruption
- Learn and implement Neuro Linguistic Programme techniques: Mirror, follow, pace and lead
- Finally, to avoid rapport becoming manipulation, be your own authentic self

Part Four. Influencing Techniques

Proposition and persuasion

"One man's meat is another man's poison."

Unknown

The successful use of positive influencing to make a proposal or to persuade others to do things hinges on an understanding of people, what moderates their behaviour, what motivates them or 'makes them tick'. This information can be gained by using the listening and questioning techniques described earlier and then used as a lever to hook into what concerns people and to provide the incentive for action, buying into your ideas etc.

- ♦ Here are just a few examples of factors that moderate, control and motivate the behaviour of individuals:
    - ❖ Habits, which are often controlled and based upon previous experience
    - ❖ Timing: On some occasions it is simply not a good time for someone

to do something. Alternatively, the moment might just be right

- ❖ Degree of capability with respect to self-awareness and understanding of the world around them
- ❖ Level of alertness, concern for the matter in hand or level of interest
- ❖ The sum of experiences that have shaped personality and character
- ❖ Everyone has a set of beliefs about themselves and the world around them. Often these are convictions that are accepted as true or real even without any tangible evidence. For example, *'I'm attractive'* or *'I'm so ugly'*
- ❖ Learned or innate behaviours. For example, likes to be at the centre of attention, needs to be praised, fears

criticism, expects to be treated in a particular way, defensive as a means to keep people at bay etc.

❖ Conscious conduct evoked in the light of circumstances or consequences. For example, acts to avoid perceived punishment such as the experience of failure or a sense of having to do something such as staying in an unsuitable job in order to meet external obligations. Conversely, an individual may seek to realise rewards which may be deemed as pleasure, the satisfaction of a need such as recognition or avoidance of anything that is going to cause pain or distress

❖ A need for affection, relationships

with colleagues and friends. A sense of belonging and the respect of others

- ❖ A need for personal growth, achievement and the attainment of goals
- ❖ The 'evidence of the crowd' or 'social proofing'. This is behaviour that is shaped by the example of others, particularly where an individual feels a sense of shared identity with the protagonist: *'If s/he is doing it, then I'm going to do it'*
- ❖ Competitiveness: Caring about social standing, acquisition of possessions, achievement etc. in relation to peers or nearest neighbours such as 'Keeping up with the Joneses'

- ❖ A need for wealth, prestige or advancement
- ❖ Desire to be in the service of others
- ❖ Motivation to meet basic needs such as sufficient resources to ensure a safe, comfortable and secure existence
- ❖ Simple likes and dislikes

When you appreciate those issues that are motivating factors, the underlying things that people or organisations etc. want, you are in a position to see life through their eyes. Furthermore, with this level of analysis you can identify the points regarding your proposal that are likely to appeal and use this knowledge to help individuals not only to see something for what it is, namely a description of the facts or the features but to recognise the benefits of your proposition. In other words, to help them to see beyond facts or features but **to see what's in it for them.**

- With underlying knowledge, you can appeal to a person's rational or emotional side and help them to see **the benefits** that they will derive from taking a proposed course of action etc. What it does, what are its effects, what they can get out of whether it is:
    - ❖ An idea
    - ❖ A plan
    - ❖ A situation
    - ❖ A service
    - ❖ A product
    - ❖ A presentation
    - ❖ A scheme
    - ❖ A purchase
- In light of what you know is a driving

stated or perceived surface requirements, rather than just persuade by means of explaining the facts or features relating to your proposal, you can make suggestions which **highlight the benefits** and you can do this by using a simple linking phrase: *'which means that…'* For example, if you were suggesting to a friend during a shopping trip in town that you stop at the nearby café for a coffee, you could factually state the price of a cup of coffee, that it is hot and comes in a cup (these are relevant features to the cup of coffee) but to influence their decision in joining you, intangible benefits related to a cup of coffee are much more relevant. For example, dependent upon your understanding of the time they have available, whether or not they have already had a break etc. you might suggest that **this means that** it would be nice to stop awhile, rest your legs and have a proper chit-chat while you watch the world go by

- Features and facts only describe what something is. Benefits (grounded in reality), allow you to persuade an individual based upon those motivators that they can relate to. Enabling people to see beyond the obvious, allowing you to personalise your proposition and to persuade by being relevant to meet individualistic needs. Therefore, while avoiding a scattergun approach (which may diminish your credibility), present the:
  - ❖ The advantages
  - ❖ It's potential
  - ❖ The benefits

- When making proposals, it may be fitting to use your understanding of rapport and persuade by using words such as *'we'* and *'you'*. If appropriate signify that you are *'in this together'*, be it the situation, the environment or marketplace. And to ensure that you are not involved in a guessing game ask questions such as *'What would you like to see happen?' 'What would doing x mean to you?'*

- Present your proposal such as an individual (individuals) understand how they can:
    - ❖ Work with it
    - ❖ Contribute to it
    - ❖ Engage with it
    - ❖ Shape it

- Persuade and create further insight by:
  - Putting ideas into context by comparing to earlier events or examples
  - Helping people to understand that they own the solution
  - Emphasising key messages

- Ethical influencing is also about giving people the opportunity to make informed personal choices. Therefore, as well as identifying benefits, individuals should be provided with any other additional information which may impact upon their final decision regarding the proposal:
  - The rationale for the proposal
  - Limits of the proposal
  - Threats

- ❖ Risks
- ❖ Serious or even grave consequences

  But
- ❖ Don't be falsely pessimistic

  And
- ❖ Don't be overly optimistic and create unrealistic expectations

To the Point

Part Four. Influencing Techniques

Information

When you possess information or particular skills you gain influence as these give you credibility. You are likely to become the person that people seek out as the 'go to person' and may even become indispensable. Credibility creates a high level of reassurance to others and this can be tied together with being trustworthy and reliable. This is illustrated when we consider people who are typically sought out on the basis of expertise. For example, surgeons, scientists, statisticians, meteorologists etc

Generally speaking the process of gaining credibility, reputation and in turn influence through the possession of information and/or skills is often a long one and usually requires consistent, excellent, hard work.

- ♦ Create credibility:

- ❖ Educate yourself
- ❖ Focus on a particular area of specialism
- ❖ Establish a record of accomplishment and achievement
- ❖ Make known the things that you have done
- ❖ Publicise the organisations, institutions, companies you have worked for, either paid or unpaid
- ❖ Publicise the awards that you have won
- ❖ Communicate your experience
- ❖ Maintain, develop and keep building upon your specialist or technical knowledge and expertise

- ♦ When presenting information to others ensure that it is:

- ❖ Accurate
- ❖ Relevant
- ❖ Objective
- ❖ Compelling
- ❖ Irrefutable

- When providing information, as appropriate, present it:
    - ❖ Within a framework which is accessible and meaningful
    - ❖ By tapping into emotions
    - ❖ By tapping into rational motivations
    - ❖ With reassurance
    - ❖ By using analogies and stories to aide understanding and create a picture
    - ❖ By describing how the future might look in light of information

> "Information is power. Disinformation is abuse of power."

Newton Lee

Part Five. Personal Positive Power to Create Influence

Character and charisma

"Whenever you do a thing act as if the whole world were watching."

Thomas Jefferson

Character is revealed through an expression of traits, habits and behaviours which communicate the nature and moral force of a person.

- You can develop your character by:
    - Looking inwards and heightening personal self-awareness. This might be achieved through the use of assessments, with therapy, during appraisals and feedback, by taking tests, enjoying challenges etc.
    - Properly examining issues for personal change. For example, asking yourself whether you are really connected with who or what you want to influence? Are you doing what you really want to do? Are you really happy?
    - Investing in yourself and so feeling

good about yourself. This in turn will enable you to generate energy and endurance which will put you in a position to positively support and influence others. You can invest in yourself through exercise and with relaxation, by keeping your knowledge and skills up to date and by maintaining relationships and networks of support

- Set an example and act as a role model for others, be:
    - Respectful
    - Competent
    - Considerate
    - Courageous
    - Curious
    - Determined

- ❖ Enthusiastic
- ❖ Focussed
- ❖ Patient
- ❖ Even tempered
- ❖ Prepared to speak
- ❖ Prepared to resolve conflict

Charisma describes those nebulous extraordinary qualities that are sometimes hard to pin down but can have the power to influence others and may even inspire enthusiasm and devotion. In certain cases, charisma can be generated by creating an air of mystery by holding back from revealing all about oneself. Alternatively, charisma may sometimes be associated with eccentricity. Unfortunately, there are occasions when individuals have used the power of charisma to emotionally cleave others to their cause or ideology resulting in catastrophic outcomes.

Charisma is often considered to be innate with people described as being naturally charming etc. However, when a baby is born while it may be described as adorable, sweet or as a little cherub etc. it would be rare to hear of a newly born infant being described as charismatic. While the word charisma can be endowed with mystical connotations which are often considered outside of the usual realm of human behaviour, many of the traits displayed by charismatic people are those that can be learned. Indeed, the performance of some well-known charismatic people such as Muhamad Ali, Marilyn Monroe and Usain Bolt display a playfulness likely to have been successfully mastered through positive reinforcement as they followed their respective paths.

- ♦ Typical words and phrases associated with

or used to describe someone with charisma:

- ❖ Enigmatic
- ❖ S/he lights up the room
- ❖ Sparkle, glowing, radiant
- ❖ Shines brightly
- ❖ Spiritual
- ❖ Dashing
- ❖ Charming
- ❖ Alluring
- ❖ Magnetic
- ❖ Has a gift
- ❖ A certain je ne sais quoi
- ❖ Wow factor, 'it' factor, 'X' factor

- ♦ You can develop your own personal charisma by considering and working on:
  - ❖ Your own sense of self awareness and confidence: Use techniques including positive self-talk or

identify and keep in mind those times when you felt really good: Think about how you sounded, what you looked like and the sensations you experienced. By continuously engaging in such positive reflection you are likely to improve your chances of feeling confident and self-assured

❖ Your demeanour: Display confidence in your posture, how you carry yourself and how you walk: Stand or sit tall, shoulders back, walk with purpose. Engage people with eye contact and of course (as appropriate to the situation) a warm smile goes a very long way

❖ How you use your voice, what you

say and how you say it. (Combining those techniques described earlier such as using assertiveness, building rapport, describing features and benefits, making appealing propositions and presenting convincing information which embody people's wants, hopes and needs)

❖ How you dress and the image you are conveying. You may wish to stand out from the crowd or use more subtle signals as discussed earlier such as the cut, fit or clean appearance of your clothes. For some individuals, continuously re-inventing their appearance provides a draw for other people and a boost to their charisma

- Personal hygiene: How you smell, and look can have a very powerful effect upon other people's desire to be in your presence. The smell of bad breath, stale cigarettes, alcohol or body odour are likely to be to your detriment
- The 'Act as If' principle developed by the Psychologist William James. He argued that if you decide to act in a particular way either by emulating someone that you regard as a role model or by choosing to adopt certain behaviours, if you keep acting as such then the act will become a habit, in turn creating inner confidence and radiating strength

- Demonstrate authenticity and build trust with character and charisma:
  - Use people's names and ensure that you use them correctly
  - Be genuinely attentive during interactions with others. Don't interrupt people when they are talking instead put them at the very heart of the conversation
  - Ensure that you are reliable, only make promises you can keep and then keep to commitments
  - Be consistent in your views
  - Even if you are experiencing extreme provocation, don't lose your temper
  - Don't be the constant defeatist or pessimist
  - Show loyalty to others. Have their

best interests at heart and have their back
- ❖ Demonstrate tact towards individuals: Ignore any embarrassing faux pas equally don't engage in offensive or personally directed humour
- ❖ Develop cultural sensitivity
- ❖ Behave with integrity. For example, avoid negative gossip. Avoid negative unjustified criticism. Be sensitive to other people by acknowledging them rather than ignoring them
- ❖ Exhibit reciprocity
- ❖ Show kindness and warmth
- ❖ Provide encouragement and give sincere compliments
- ❖ Make people feel special

Part Six. Concluding the Influencing Process

Gaining commitment and handling objections

"Integrity has no need of rules."

Albert Camus

Influencing may form part of an ongoing relationship. For example, no sooner than they are elected, American Presidents are quickly back out on the campaign trail. A leader needs to maintain influence as does anyone in a management role. However, there are other occasions when influence is part of a short-term communication, perhaps to make a one-off sale or direct somebody to a service. Therefore, you may seek to gain evidence of commitment to your ideas etc. In certain situation this may be about 'signing on the dotted line'. It may be the case that just by asking and checking if someone is onboard will be enough to obtain affirmation or a promise to your proposal. On the other hand, to reinforce commitment both in the mind of individuals and for your own personal assurance you can use questioning to test genuine undertakings towards your suggestions.

- Questions to test commitment and elicit a firm decision:
  - Assuming commitment. For example, *'What's your next step going to be?' 'How soon will you be doing x?' 'How will you explain your decision to your partner?' 'What do you think you will get out of this?' 'What other information do you want?' 'What do you think will happen when you do x?'*
  - Limiting the alternatives: For example, *'Would you prefer to have lunch on Tuesday or Wednesday?' 'Which of the options available is the one that you are going to take?'*

- To help people to commit to your proposal(s) ensure that you have:
  - Not put them under undue

pressure

❖ Not harassed them by telling them what they should think or feel by using phrases such as *'You'd better not...' 'You ought to...' 'You're wrong...' 'You should...'*

❖ Listened and identified all of their needs

❖ Addressed any doubts

❖ Given them sufficient and accurate information (which they may not only need for themselves but to allow them to convince others of benefits etc. such as their partner, colleagues or friends)

❖ Been honest with them

You might feel confident that someone is committed to your influence if they engage with you by asking questions, show interest with their body language such as nodding in agreement, making statements such as *'I can see how it will be of use'*, writing things down or positively relating the options you may have provided to their own circumstances. On the other hand, some people may raise objections, or it may be the case that you believe someone has been too quick to say yes to your suggestions or that what they are saying to you contains inconsistencies. In these situations, you may wish to confront the genuineness of their commitment or handle the objection. While this may seem a challenge, treat it as an opportunity to head off a potential problem area, to alleviate doubts and resolve any concerns.

- Earlier, confronting the negative impact of behaviour was discussed when exploring assertiveness. Confronting or handling objections within the context of commitment is about:

- ❖ Making explicit any disconnect between what you hear the other person saying they are going to do but which would appear to be incongruent with body language or other signals. For example, agreeing by saying *'Yeah, yeah, yeah'* but it is said in such a way as to appear disinterested or dismissive
- ❖ Highlighting differences between what you want to do and what they want to do
- ❖ Highlighting differences between their values and your values
- ❖ Highlighting matters where you feel someone is not being truthful with you

- ❖ Raising matters when you feel that someone is trying to hide their real motivations or feelings
- ❖ Addressing reticence
- ❖ Addressing aggressive behaviour
- ❖ Correcting misunderstandings
- ❖ In light of your new proposals, helping someone to overcome previous experience (be it real or perceived as real)
- ❖ Confronting unrealistic aims or expectations
- ❖ Confronting matters when someone is asking for too much

- ♦ When you handle objections or confront or raise issues you can risk 'putting people on the back foot' in which case they might feel hurt, threatened, angry or on the defensive.

Therefore, you should be tentative and supportive:

- Don't take things personally, you can't win them all
- Maintain a positive attitude
- Be thoughtful and considered before you reply
- Tackle the issue, not the person. Don't say things like *'You're always like this!'*
- Check that you have heard and understood correctly *'So what you want is...' 'So, what you are worried about is...'*
- If an objection is raised, say *'Thank you for raising the issue' 'I appreciate you bringing that up'* etc
- If an objection is based on previous experience, find out exactly what

happened and why
- ❖ Whether an objection is valid or not, explore compensating factors by selling the benefits
- ❖ Look out for multiple objections and deal with them one at a time
- ❖ As appropriate, you could suggest that the individual makes a list of their objections and that you address them one at a time
- ❖ If someone is raising spurious objections or trying to stall things or create a smokescreen, you may wish to say something like *'Putting that to one side, what other reasons do you have…?*
- ❖ On some occasions you may need to ask someone to delay their objection and leave it with you so that you

can come back to them
- ❖ Acknowledge their point of view
- ❖ Check that they understand you and your position
- ❖ Put objections into perspective
- ❖ Don't argue
- ❖ Don't make it look like you've heard it all before
- ❖ Don't try to score points
- ❖ Suggest alternatives
- ❖ Acknowledge that you may have differing opinions, views, solutions etc.
- ❖ Make certain that people have information about the potential consequences of their choices
- ❖ Be empathetic, what might be right for you may not be right for them
- ❖ Don't collude in people's negativity

or despondency

- ❖ Using an assertive approach, ask for their preferred solution and engage in joint problem solving
- ❖ Check that things have been resolved before moving on
- ❖ Remind yourself that ultimately, people have responsibility for their own choices

Part Six. Concluding the Influencing Process

Disengaging and ending

> *"You can lead a horse to water, but you cannot make it drink."*

Unknown

Disengaging or ending the influencing approach

- There are occasions when it may be appropriate to suspend or cease attempts to influence:
    - ❖ You have reached the limits of what you can do
    - ❖ Desired outcomes are looking unlikely
    - ❖ New information comes to light
    - ❖ There may be a need to reduce pressure
    - ❖ Emotions are running high
    - ❖ The relationship is in danger of being damaged
    - ❖ Time may be required to think things through
    - ❖ It is realised that influence may only be achieved if given space and time.

Therefore, look to create a series of events, meetings etc

- Ending the influencing approach:
  - Goals and objectives have been achieved
  - Mutual understanding has been achieved
  - Support has been obtained
  - You have handled objections
  - You have fulfilled desired outcomes
  - Agreement has been tested out and commitment confirmed
  - As necessary, future action has been established

Note

The contents of this book have been designed to help you to create influence across different circumstances with different people. However, it is worth noting that influencing is a skill mastered over a period of time and which takes measured application. Create a self-improvement plan, envisage what you will look like, sound like and feel like when you have achieved your goals.

Good Luck

Prepare, practice
&
Be a positive influence in the world

To the Point

About the Author

Jacqueline Mansell Chartered FCIPD., FSET., is a Chartered Psychologist and business owner who has worked in a career dedicated to learning and development.

During the course of her career Jacqueline has reached many people through her work and interventions and is now bringing her accumulated knowledge and expertise to a wider audience through her handbooks.

To the Point handbooks have been designed by Jacqueline to provide a compilation of her reference notes and presentation materials, built over the span of many years. The handbooks cover psychological themes accessible and applicable to everyday living.

To the Point

www.ingramcontent.com/pod-product-compliance
Lightning Source LLC
Chambersburg PA
CBHW071435080526
44587CB00014B/1857